Why Christians Should

SPEAK in TONGUES

Why Christians Should

SPEAK in TONGUES

PRAYING WITH SUPERNATURALLY CHARGED
POWER AND EFFECTIVENESS

GORDON LINDSAY

This book is a compilation and revision of Volumes 1-4 of *The Gifts of the Spirit* by Gordon Lindsay.

DESTINY IMAGE® PUBLISHERS, INC.
PO Box 310, Shippensburg, PA 17257-0310
"Publishing cutting-edge prophetic resources to supernaturally empower the body of Christ"

This book and all other Destiny Image and Destiny Image Fiction books are available at Christian bookstores and distributors worldwide.

For more information on foreign distributors, call 717-532-3040.
Reach us on the Internet: www.destinyimage.com.

ISBN 13 TP: 978-0-7684-7298-1
ISBN 13 eBook: 978-0-7684-7442-8

For Worldwide Distribution.
1 2 3 4 5 6 7 8 / 28 27 26 25 24

CONTENTS

INTRODUCTION

The gifts of the Spirit are among the most important topics in the New Testament. In 1 Corinthians 12:27, Paul reveals the Church as the Body of Christ. He explains that the members of this Body are believers exercising various gifts, just as the parts of the human body have different functions and purposes. Paul adds that all members working harmoniously together become the supernatural Body of Christ on earth.

In light of this, it follows that without the gifts of the Spirit, the Church would become something quite different from that which God intended. Rather than a supernatural organism, the Church would be only another human organization. We know from the historical record that shortly after the early apostolic era, the gifts of the Spirit started to gradually disappear from the Church. Why? One common explanation is that when the New Testament canon was completed, they were no longer needed. The well-known writer, Donald Gee, pointed out in his book, *Concerning Spiritual Gifts,* no evidence is found to support this opinion. He writes:

> Such an argument rests upon a complete misconception of the true nature and purpose of the Gifts of the Spirit. It assumes that in the Early Church, utterances through these gifts had all the authority of the Scriptures, but the New Testament utterly disproves such an idea. The Early Church is consistently found always appealing to the Scriptures of the Old Testament (never to their own "prophets" be it noted), for support for all doctrine and final settlement in every dispute (Acts 2:16, 15:15, 26:22). The "prophecy of Scripture" provided (2 Peter 1:20) a totally different level of authority to

the spiritual gifts among them, and it does so still.[1]

Although the manifestation of the gifts widely ceased after the apostolic age, no evidence has been found that this occurred because the Lord withdrew them. It appears that they ceased because the Church became lukewarm.

> *Nevertheless I have this against you, that you have left your first love. Remember therefore from where you have fallen; repent and do the first works, or else I will come to you quickly and remove your lampstand from its place—unless you repent* (Revelation 2:4-5).

While the operation of the gifts greatly diminished over the ensuing centuries of the church age, they did not entirely disappear. And when believers began to earnestly pray for their restoration to the Church, the present, latter-day outpourings of the Spirit resulted.

NOTE

1   Donald Gee, *Concerning Spiritual Gifts, Revised and Enlarged Edition* (Springfield, MO: Gospel Publishing House, 1937), 11.

CHAPTER 1

21 REASONS CHRISTIANS SHOULD SPEAK IN TONGUES

1. Speaking in other tongues is foretold in the Old Testament prophecies. (Isaiah 28:11-12)

It has been well said that the Old Testament is the New concealed, and the New Testament is the Old revealed. All the great truths of the New Testament have their roots in the Old. Therefore, it is not surprising that the phenomenon of speaking in other tongues is clearly foretold in Isaiah, a book written some 800 years before the Church Age began.

The law of first mention involves the particular fact that when a great truth first appears in Scripture, the most important aspects about the truth are mentioned or touched upon in the passage. In this regard, the following important points are alluded to in the prophecy:

- This fulfillment of this prophecy would take place in its fullness just before the end of the age. Notice that it is associated with the powerful end-of-the-age prophecies.

- Speaking in other tongues will be a special means by which God will reach people during this particular time.

- Speaking in other tongues includes stammering lips, inferring that at first the utterances may be halting and broken before the clear flow of the language comes forth.

- This phenomenon of speaking in other tongues will be directly associated with a special "refreshing" and "rest" that God will give to His people—a blessing that is the baptism of the Holy Spirit.

- Despite the manifestation of this divine phenomenon, many harden their hearts, reject it, and in turn are rejected by God. The extreme danger of this type of unbelief is shown in Isaiah 28:12-13.

2. The New Testament declares that speaking in tongues is a fulfillment of Old Testament prophecy. (1 Corinthians 14:21)

The prophecy in Isaiah was not overlooked in the New Testament. When the apostle Paul discussed the various gifts of the Spirit in his first epistle to the Corinthians, he pointed out that this prophecy foretold the coming gift of tongues to the New Testament Church. He added that the prophecy mentioned one of the great purposes of the gift. It should be a sign to unbelievers.

3. In the Great Commission, Christ said believers should speak in tongues. (Mark 16:15-17)

One of the most important passages in the Bible is Mark 16, where Christ gave the Great Commission to the Church. They are the last words of our Lord before He returned to Heaven. The tremendous importance of these words has been universally recognized by the Church down through the centuries. The Church was to go into all the world and preach the Gospel and make disciples of all nations. The fact that Jesus included speaking in other tongues in the Great Commission emphatically calls attention to its importance.

4. The original 120 disciples who were filled with the Holy Spirit on the Day of Pentecost spoke with other tongues.

The original members of the early Church were those 120 who obeyed the Lord's command to *"tarry in the*

*city of Jerusalem until you are endued with power
from on high"* (Luke 24:49). These believers included
the apostles, perhaps the 70, Mary, the mother of Jesus,
and certain others (Acts 1:14). The Day of Pentecost
came, and the Holy Spirit suddenly fell upon them,
and each person began to speak in other tongues!
(Acts 2:1-4) A supernatural visitation revival broke
out that day and before night, 3,000 souls accepted
Christ.

5. The first Gentiles to be saved received the Holy Spirit and spoke in other tongues.

The story of Cornelius and how his household was
saved and received the Holy Spirit holds a prominent
place in the Book of Acts. Although even the apostles
did not understand it, God's plan was for both Jews and
Gentiles to share in the blessings of the New Testament
era that were obtained through Christ's death and res-
urrection (Acts 10:44-45).

6. The apostle Paul spoke in other tongues.

The apostle Paul was an outstanding figure in the early Church. His conversion was most unusual. Brought up a strict Pharisee, his intellectual powers promised a brilliant future in the Jewish religion—before his extraordinary experience on the Damascus Road (Acts 9). At that moment, his whole life was changed. Paul received the Holy Spirit and was delivered from blindness. Paul later wrote, *"I thank my God I speak with tongues more than you all"* (1 Corinthians 14:18). Paul's experience is significant as a pattern for all Christians who believe in Christ (1 Timothy 1:16).

7. More than 25 years after Pentecost, those who received the Holy Spirit spoke in other tongues.

More than 25 years after the Day of Pentecost, Paul went to Ephesus on one of his many missionary journeys. Upon meeting some disciples from that city, he asked, *"Did you receive the Holy Spirit when you believed?"* (Acts 19:2). Paul found that they knew only about John's baptism.

Paul then preached a sermon on the Holy Spirit (Matthew 3:11). These disciples, upon accepting Paul's report, were baptized in water. Paul then laid hands upon them and they received the baptism of the Holy Spirit and spoke in other tongues! (Acts 19:6)

8. Did the believers in Samaria who received the Holy Spirit speak in other tongues?

Only one other time does the New Testament record that people received the Holy Spirit (Acts 8:17). It does not specifically record that they spoke in other tongues but notice what happened in Acts 8:4-25 when Simon, a sorcerer, attended a revival where people were filled with the Holy Spirit, they spoke in other tongues. This phenomenon astonished Simon.

9. Speaking in other tongues is a gift given by God to the Church, the Body of Christ.

In 1 Corinthians 12, Paul lists nine gifts given by the Holy Spirit to the Church. Among these gifts is speaking in different kinds of tongues (1 Corinthians 12:10). God has never withdrawn these gifts from the Church. The only Scripture offered in an effort to substantiate such a position is found in 1 Corinthians 13:8. The context, however, clearly shows that this is not Paul's meaning. He is referring to the time *"when that which is perfect has come"* (1 Corinthians 13:10). Until that time, speaking in other tongues and all the other manifestations of the Holy Spirit are necessary just as Jesus said in the Great Commission (Mark 16:17).

10. God has set different kinds of tongues in the Church.

The sign of speaking in tongues apparently follows as the initial evidence of the baptism of the Holy Spirit. However, beyond this, God gives to some believers a more varied manifestation of the gift—the ability to speak not only one tongue, but in "different tongues" (1 Corinthians 12:7-11). The specialized "varieties of tongues" gift is for certain individuals chosen by the Spirit (1 Corinthians 12:28-30).

11. Those who speak in other tongues speak to God. (1 Corinthians 14:2)

At the time of conversion, God speaks to us in our language, "Child, you are now a member of My family." When we are baptized in the Holy Spirit, we are able to speak, as it were, to God in His language—a language only He understands. If God chooses, He can give us a language that not even the devil can understand—a way of communicating with God that neither people nor the devil can intercept.

12. The believer who speaks in tongues edifies himself. (1 Corinthians 14:4)

Naturally, individuals cannot understand how it can be a blessing or how they are edified by it until they speak in tongues. Once they receive it, they find that it is a supernatural experience carrying with it a rich spiritual blessing.

13. Paul said, "I wish you all spoke with tongues" (1 Corinthians 14:5).

Not all gifts of the Spirit are for every believer to exercise. Yet, the gift of speaking in other tongues is of such nature that all who exercise it may edify themselves. Paul found the gift highly profitable in his devotions and prayer life (1 Corinthians 14:15,18).

14. If interpreted, speaking in tongues is equal to prophecy. (1 Corinthians 14:5)

If the Holy Spirit enables either the one who speaks in tongues or another person present to interpret the message given, the Church is edified. When these two gifts function together, they are equal to the gift of prophecy.

15. One may pray in the Spirit through an unknown tongue. (Romans 8:26-27)

When we are at a loss for words to express ourselves in prayer, the Holy Spirit will, in the unknown tongue, take the need and lift it up to God. With the Holy Spirit praying through us, all things will work for our good (Romans 8:28).

16. Speaking in tongues is a sign to unbelievers. (1 Corinthians 14:21-22)

Although some people resent speaking in other tongues, many can testify that they were first spiritually awakened by the manifestation of this sign. Though they did not understand all about it, they sensed that God was in it. Others may have heard a message in tongues with the interpretation that followed and knew it was God's voice speaking to them.

17. Speaking in other tongues sometimes has been in the native language of someone present, causing them to believe the reality of the gift.

The power of speaking in other tongues is multiplied many times when the language used is known to one or more of the listeners. In almost every case like this, the listeners are amazed and astonished to hear a message in their language from the lips of someone they know has never learned the language (Acts 2:5-6).

18. God said that with stammering lips and another tongue He would speak to the people.

When Isaiah 28 mentioned speaking in other tongues, it included the sign of "stammering lips" (Isaiah 28:11). This sign has often been a stumbling block to certain people.

When the Holy Spirit comes upon you, do not be fearful. Do not suppress the Holy Spirit or stifle the stammering lips. Let God have His way. As you learn to speak and as you yield to His Spirit, the stammering lips will change to a beautiful, fluent flow of language.

19. Speaking in other tongues is an indication of rest and refreshing promised by the Lord. (Isaiah 28:12)

When the Holy Spirit comes, He speaks. This manifestation and presence of the Holy Spirit is accompanied by speaking in other tongues; likewise "rest and refreshing" is accompanied by the presence of the Spirit (Acts 3:19). Speaking in other tongues indicates the presence of the Holy Spirit, who has come to make His home in the believer's life.

20. Paul commanded the Church not to forbid to speak with tongues. (1 Corinthians 14:39)

In summing up his instructions on speaking in other tongues, Paul charged the church, *"do not forbid to speak with tongues.*" Paul knew that the exercise of the gift in the assembly would cause problems and that undisciplined people would sometimes misuse the gift, like they did in the Corinthian Church. Yet he did not consider these possible dangers sufficient to rule out speaking in other tongues (1 Corinthians 13:1; 14:38-40).

21. The contrast between the Tower of Babel and Pentecost.

At the Tower of Babel, God sent judgment on the irreverent builders by confusing their languages (Genesis 11:5-9). On the Day of Pentecost, God set the gift of speaking in other tongues in the Church so people from the scattered nations could hear and understand the wonderful works of God. At Babel, the builders were confused and forced to stop building their pagan temple. At Pentecost, God began building a new structure—the Church of the Living God, with Jesus Christ as the Chief Cornerstone (Acts 4:11).

Thank God for the gift of speaking in tongues. It has become one of the great channels by which individuals are united with God (1 Corinthians 14:2).

CHAPTER 2

HOW TO RECEIVE THE HOLY SPIRIT BAPTISM

By Mrs. Gordon Lindsay

Life is filled with complex problems. That is a fact that no one would challenge. What is the answer? Has God created mankind upon this Earth to be continually abused and buffeted by the enemy? No, God has given us an appropriate weapon—the baptism of the Holy Spirit. With this, you can become the *answer* in your home, your church, your community. Without it, you will part of the *problem*.

Who is to receive the Holy Spirit? Paul says in Ephesians 5:18, *"Be filled with the Spirit."* This includes every boy and girl, every man and woman, as the Lord told us in Joel 2:28-29.

It sounds as if God didn't leave anybody out. We have been witnesses to this fact. God's Spirit is being poured out around the world on people, and not only on great people, but also upon servants. We have seen the Lord baptize children at three years of age, and we have witnessed Him fill those who are 100 years old. We have seen Him fill the Lutheran, Methodist, Baptist, Assembly of God, Muslim, Hindu, Mormon, Indian, and Catholic (Luke 11:13).

The infilling of the Holy Spirit is an experience subsequent to salvation. It is a distinct and separate gift, as shown in Acts 19:1-6. Whether it is one, two, or three days after your conversion, the important thing is to be filled with the Spirit now.

Tongues have not been done away with, as some teach from 1 Corinthians 13:8-9. There has never been a time when there was as much knowledge as there is today!

WHAT IS THE PURPOSE OF THE HOLY SPIRIT?

Acts 1:8 informs us that we receive power after the Holy Spirit comes upon us. Power to live an overcoming life, power to pray for the sick, power for the service of our Master.

Acts 1:8 also tells us the Holy Spirit shall make us witnesses. The Holy Spirit is a flame within us that drives us to witness to the lost about this glorious Gospel.

First Corinthians 14:4 describes that when we pray in tongues we are edified—built up, energized, or charged up like a car battery.

First Corinthians 14:2 says, *"In the spirit he speaks mysteries."* In other words, we have a secret code between us and God, which the devil will never be able to crack!

John 14:26 (KJV) reveals another attribute of the Holy Spirit, the Comforter. In this world with death and sorrow, what a joy it is to possess this wonderful Comforter.

John 14:26 also gives the promise that the Holy Spirit brings to your remembrance all things that He says to you. He will invigorate our minds for the particular work the Lord calls us to do, be it secular or spiritual. Our God-given, natural abilities find their highest expression and greatest reward as we yield our lives completely to the Holy Spirit.

The infilling of the Holy Spirit broadens our world in prayer. When we pray with our understanding, we pray only for things we know. When we pray in the Spirit, God is able to lay burdens for individuals around the world upon our hearts. Praying becomes more pleasurable, and a new joy wells up within us.

Another tremendous asset of being filled with the Spirit is the rest and refreshing it brings (Isaiah 28:12)— body, soul, and spirit.

The Holy Spirit is a divinely appointed guide (John 16:13). Life does not need to be a hit-and-miss comedy of errors. How much better to commit our lives daily to the Master in prayer and let the Holy Spirit guide us.

HOW CAN ONE BE FILLED WITH THE HOLY SPIRIT?

Let's begin with the most quoted Pentecostal scripture, Acts 2:4: *"And they were all filled with the Holy Spirit and began to speak with other tongues, as the Spirit gave them utterance."* Who began to speak? Some answer, "The Holy Spirit." But that is not what the Scripture says. Read the verse again. It says, *"They* began to speak."

One might object, "If I do the speaking, it will be the flesh speaking." That's right. Joel 2:28 says He will pour out His Spirit on all flesh in the last days. As long as you have a mortal body, you will be speaking in the flesh. Once you are taken to Heaven, you won't need to speak in tongues.

This is where the supernatural comes in: *"As the Spirit gave them utterance."* If you had to think up the words to say, there would be nothing supernatural about it; but the Spirit gives you the words to say. After you have centered all your thoughts on the Lord in worship, you speak out, in faith, the words that are in your heart. You won't understand them, but that won't matter.

Don't be afraid of your voice, for the words will sound strange. They may at first sound like a child learning to speak. Isaiah 28:11 says, *"For with stammering lips and another tongue He will speak to this people."* But don't hesitate. Speak out the words distinctly. Express what God has put in your heart.

Take a deep breath and begin to speak in tongues. Remember, if you are saved, you have Christ, and Colossians 2:9 says, *"For in Him dwells all the fullness of the Godhead bodily."* Believe that you have the Holy Spirit in you. You are not waiting on God to do something for you. He is waiting for you to do something for Him.

When I speak in English, I use my tongue, lips, teeth, and voice. You must do exactly the same when you speak in tongues; use your lips, teeth, tongue, and your voice. I have seen many who are expecting to be filled with the Spirit become very tense. Their upper lip becomes rigid; they can't even speak in their own language in this fashion! Rest in the Lord. Relax and watch the beautiful Holy Spirit move in your life.

If you are capable of conversing in English, French, Spanish, and German, you could only speak one language at a time, right? Likewise, if you insist on continuing to speak in the language that is natural to you, you can pray forever, and you will never speak in tongues.

Praise the Lord for a few minutes until you feel the Holy Spirit moving in your soul. Stop speaking in your native language, and in faith begin to speak in the unknown tongue.

As you become obedient to the moving of the Holy Spirit, great joy will flood your soul, for the Bible says, *"And the disciples were filled with joy and with the*

Holy Spirit" (Acts 13:52). That joy may come the day you receive the Holy Spirit, or it may come later as you learn to submit yourself to Him.

CHAPTER 3

30 OBJECTIONS TO SPEAKING IN TONGUES AND THE BIBLICAL ANSWERS

Objection 1:

Some say that the passage of Mark 16:9-20, in which are included the words, *"they will speak with new tongues"* (verse 17), is a counterfeit addition to the Book of Mark.

Answer:

While a few manuscripts omit this passage, many more with a greater authority include it. With a few exceptions, all the Greek manuscripts have retained these 12 verses. The Cursive manuscripts unanimously recognize the passage as genuine.

The Vulgate version prepared by Jerome in an early century includes the disputed verses. Many early church fathers quote from the passage in their writings, thus further indicating its genuineness. (See Irenaeus, Against Heresies, Book III, Chapter 10.)

The internal evidence strongly indicates that the passage is a part of Mark 16. Certainly, the stark abruptness of the end of the eighth verse is almost overwhelming proof that there was something additional after it. Can we imagine Mark, the forceful evangelist, ending his book with the words, "for they were afraid"? The authenticity of the Mark 16:15-18 passage is attested ultimately by the fact that it agrees perfectly with the rest of New Testament teachings.

Objection 2:

If we are to accept Mark 16:15-18 as genuine, Christians must handle snakes to show they are true believers. For it reads, *"they will take up serpents."*

Answer:

The Bible explains its own statements. What is meant by the statement, *"they will take up serpents"*? Does it mean that Christians are to go out and literally pick up deadly snakes to prove they are believers? When Paul picked up a snake by accident (Acts 28:3-5), he did not wave it around to show he was a believer but shook it off into the fire. God protected him from its deadly bite, and he suffered no harm.

People are not to drink deadly poisons and pick up snakes to prove they are believers. If by mistake or accident they should do so, they may claim the promise of immunity. The promise of divine protection for those who believe is consistent with the Scriptures (Psalm 91).

Objection 3:

Presuming the passage of Mark 16:15-18 is genuine, the words, *"they will speak with new tongues"* must mean that, after conversion, one's speech will be from a renewed spirit. That is, instead of cursing and speaking evil as they did in the past, people will now bless others.

Answer:

It is true that God does put a new song in the mouths of His people when they are converted. However, the signs listed in the context—divine healing and casting out devils—are supernatural signs. All rules of logic require that this sign also be supernatural.

It is true that some teach that God withdrew this gift as well as others from the Church on the basis that it had served its purpose. However, there are no biblical grounds for this view.

Objection 4:

Some say speaking in an unknown tongue actually did not happen. Some contest that in every instance where the gift of tongues was granted, the onlookers or believers included foreigners who spoke different languages and could, therefore, understand what was spoken.

Answer:

Few expositors hold this view, for it is in flat contradiction to the Scriptures. It is well known that on the Day of Pentecost, people from 17 countries heard the 120 disciples speaking in their respective languages. Similar incidents have occurred in our own time, as proven by numerous witnesses. Nevertheless, the understanding of a message in other tongues by someone who happens to know the language, while not unusual, only happens occasionally.

Ordinarily, tongues are not understood by anyone present. This is clearly stated by Paul in 1 Corinthians 14:2. When speaking in other tongues occurs in a public assembly, the gift of interpretation of tongues is needed to make known what is said (1 Corinthians 14:13,27).

Objection 5:

Pentecostals teach that everyone should speak in tongues, but Paul asks the question, *"Do all speak with tongues?"* (1 Corinthians 12:30). The question implies that all do not. Therefore, the teaching that speaking in other tongues always accompanies the baptism in the Holy Spirit is inaccurate.

Answer:

What is the real meaning of the words, *"Do all speak with tongues?"* First Corinthians chapters 12 and 14 plainly refer to the gifts of the Spirit as they operate in the Church. The gift of tongues is actually "different kinds of tongues" (1 Corinthians 12:10,28). It is clear that all do not have the gift of "diversities in tongues," nor are "different kinds of tongues" associated with the infilling of the Spirit.

However, there is an aspect of speaking in tongues directly associated with receiving the Spirit. Thus, on the Day of Pentecost, every one of the 120, when filled with the Spirit, began to speak in other tongues. It should be noted that Peter associated this phenomenon with Joel's promise. When the people asked in Acts 2:12, *"Whatever could this mean?"* (speaking in other tongues), Peter related it to God's promise to pour out His Spirit upon all flesh (Acts 2:16-18).

There are obviously two phases of speaking in tongues. One is the initial evidence of the baptism; the other is the gift as listed in 1 Corinthians 12.

Objection 6:

Paul stated that tongues are a sign not to those who believe, but to those who do not. Pentecostals make it a sign to those who believe.

Answer:

Speaking in other tongues is indeed a sign to unbelievers (1 Corinthians 14:21). In the days of the early Church, speaking in other tongues was a sign of coming judgment, not to believers but to unbelievers. The prophet Isaiah pointed out that the sign would not be accepted by the nation as a whole (Isaiah 28:13).

The fulfillment of prophecy that tongues is a sign to unbelievers does not nullify its obvious meaning as a scriptural evidence of the infilling of the Holy Spirit. The apostles knew those at the house of Cornelius had received the Holy Spirit (Acts 10:46). One Scripture cannot be interpreted to contradict another.

Objection 7:

Certain Scriptures indicate that one cannot be a Christian unless they have the Holy Spirit. Many have felt the regenerating and sanctifying power of the Spirit and have never spoken in other tongues.

Answer:

All believers have a measure of the Spirit, as Paul declares in 1 Corinthians 12:3 and Romans 8:9. It is clear from these Scriptures that a person cannot be a Christian without having the Holy Spirit. Christ made a clear distinction between having the Holy Spirit and having the Spirit dwell within you in (John 14:17). It is readily agreed that all saved people have the Holy Spirit, but that does not mean there is not an additional experience of the baptism in the Spirit. The fullness of the Spirit is described in John 7:37-39.

Objection 8:

Speaking in other tongues is referred to in only one epistle. If the gift were important, Paul would have mentioned it in other epistles. That it is referred to only in 1 Corinthians, a letter written to a carnal church, proves that Paul puts a low value upon it.

Answer:

The Lord's Supper is given great emphasis by most denominations, but it is mentioned in no other epistle except 1 Corinthians, and in only one place. In contrast, speaking in other tongues is referred to no less than 18 times in the same book!

Many writers, however, believe that speaking in other tongues is referred to in other epistles: Ephesians 5:19, Colossians 3:16, and 1 Corinthians 14:15. Many commentaries consider that 1 Thessalonians 5:19-20, *"Do not quench the Spirit. Do not despise prophecies,"* refers partly to speaking in other tongues.

The gifts of the Spirit, which include speaking in other tongues, are directly referred to in Hebrews 2:4, 1 Corinthians 14:14-15, Romans 8:26, and Jesus said, *"And these signs will follow those who believe...they will speak with new tongues"* (Mark 16:17).

Objection 9:

Paul said, *"Yet in the church I would rather speak five words with my understanding, that I may teach others also, than ten thousand words in a tongue"* (1 Corinthians 14:19). According to this verse, preaching God's Word is 2,000 times as desirable as speaking in an unknown tongue.

Answer:

The verse in 1 Corinthians 14:19 must be considered in context. Paul says in 1 Corinthians 14:5 that *"he who prophesies is greater than he who speaks with tongues, unless indeed he interprets, that the church may receive edification.*" Paul is saying is that there is to be no speaking in unknown tongues in the public assembly except with interpretation. However, if there is interpretation, it is equated with prophecy. To isolate a Scripture from its context is not the way to interpret God's Word.

Objection 10:

Speaking in tongues is placed last in both lists of gifts and gift-ministries; therefore, it is the least of the gifts.

Answer:

We have never heard anyone contend that speaking in tongues is better than other gifts, but that does not mean it should not deserve full recognition. The apostle Paul compares these gifts, including speaking in other tongues, to the members of the human body. He declares that those members who are the most feeble are also necessary in (1 Corinthians 12:18-22).

It should be added that just because speaking in tongues is listed last does not necessarily mean it is the least. In 1 Corinthians 13, tongues is mentioned before prophecy, but this does not mean it is greater than prophecy. The objection that the gift of tongues is inconsequential because it is mentioned last has no weight at all.

Objection 11:

Speaking in other tongues on the Day of Pentecost was to make possible the rapid evangelization of the world. When this work was completed, the gift of tongues was no longer necessary.

Answer:

It is true that this particular manifestation of the gift of tongues occurred on the Day of Pentecost. However, evangelization was not the main purpose; in fact, it is the exception not the rule. When Paul explains the varied purposes of the gifts of the Spirit in 1 Corinthians

14, he begins his discussion by saying, *"For he who speaks in a tongue does not speak to men but to God, for no one understands him"* (1 Corinthians 14:2).

It is a historical fact that Greek, Aramaic, and Latin were the principal languages spoken in the Roman world, therefore it was possible for the early Church to evangelize to the nations with a minimum of language barriers.

Objection 12:

The gifts of the Spirit, including speaking in other tongues, were needed to establish Christianity. After this was accomplished, the gifts were no longer needed.

Answer:

To imply that the entire world now believes in Christianity and that the ministry of the supernatural is no longer needed is to merely shut one's eyes to reality. Islam is having a revival. Hinduism, Buddhism, and

Confucianism have vast followings. If anything, the need for the supernatural is greater now than ever before.

Objection 13:

Even though the sign-gifts appeared in the early Church, historically their manifestation did diminish greatly near the end of the first century. This indicates that God's purpose for them was largely fulfilled, and He was withdrawing them.

Answer:

The argument that the Lord was responsible for the disappearance of the Church's spiritual gifts is without scriptural foundation. When Jesus gave the Great Commission to the apostles, He said that signs would follow those who believe. The church of Ephesus began with a revival in which speaking in tongues was manifested. When the gifts declined in the church, it was because they lost their first love (Revelation 2:4-5).

Objection 14:

The apostle Paul says in 1 Corinthians 13:8,10, *"whether there are tongues, they will cease...But when that which is perfect has come, then that which is in part will be done away."* This means that when the New Testament canon was completed, there was no further need for this gift.

Answer:

This passage says that prophecy, tongues, and knowledge shall vanish away. Those who oppose speaking in tongues advance the idea that the words "when that which is perfect has come" refer to the New Testament canon. But a careful look at the context shows that Paul is not referring to the New Testament canon at all, but to the perfect age (1 Corinthians 13:12). The word "then" clearly refers to the time when we shall see Christ face to face. The gifts of the Spirit, speaking in tongues, and the gift of prophecy stopped. Only when God's redemption plan is complete, everyone will return to a "pure language" (Zephaniah 3:9). At that time the divine judgment given at Babel will be lifted and speaking in tongues will cease.

Objection 15:

One of the groups of people who heard the disciples speaking in other tongues on the Day of Pentecost were residents of Judea. Since the disciples, who were Galileans, spoke Aramaic, the same language as the Judeans, it follows that some of the disciples must have spoken supernaturally in their own language rather than in other tongues. That being true, not all 120 spoke in other tongues.

Answer:

To say the Galileans spoke in their own dialect is to contradict the Scriptures, which state that *all spoke in other tongues*. Although the Galilean and Judean tongues were similar, the Galilean was a distinctly different dialect from the Judean. This was seen when Peter tried to hide his identity at the time he was denying Jesus. His accusers said to him, *"You are a Galilean, and your speech shows it"* (Mark 14:70). It was impossible for the Galileans to speak without their peculiar accent. This is why the Judeans were amazed that they spoke in the Judean dialect (Acts 2:4). That means that all 120 spoke in other tongues.

Objection 16:

Some Pentecostals refer to speaking in tongues as the initial evidence of the baptism in the Holy Spirit. However, the baptism in the Holy Spirit occurred at Pentecost when the Spirit fell upon the Church. Never again do the Scriptures speak of anyone being baptized in the Spirit. It occurred once and for all at Pentecost.

Answer:

This statement is incorrect. The Scriptures refer to those at the house of Cornelius receiving the "same gift" (Acts 11:17) that the disciples received at Pentecost, and even spoke of their experience as *"baptized with the Holy Spirit"* (Acts 11:16). Those accompanying Peter to Cornelius' house knew that the Gentiles had received the Holy Spirit, *"For they heard them speak with tongues and magnify God"* (Acts 10:46).

We can see several things from this passage: 1) The Gentiles spoke with tongues, proving to the Jews that they had received the Holy Spirit; 2) they received it the same way the 120 did at the beginning, on the Day of Pentecost; 3) it was the "same gift" the apostles had received.

Objection 17:

Nothing is said about the Samaritans speaking in tongues when they received the Holy Spirit (Acts 8:1-25).

Answer:

Carl Brumback, in his classic book *What Meaneth This?* answers this question so clearly that it can scarcely be improved upon.

Verses 18 and 19 tell us, *"And when Simon saw that through laying on of the apostles' hands the Holy Ghost was given, he offered them money, saying, 'Give me also this power also, that on whomsoever I lay hands, he may receive the Holy Ghost.'"* No one can doubt from these words that there was an outward evidence of the reception of the Spirit. It does not seem plausible that a man of Simon's caliber would offer money for the ability to produce an invisible effect.

What, then, did Simon see? It is our conviction that Simon witnessed the glossolalia. This miracle of utterance was entirely new to him, and would arrest his attention as nothing else. How he would covet the power to impart this gift!

The voice they uttered was awful in its range, in its tones, in its modulation, in its startling, almost penetrating power; the words they spoke were exalted, intense, passionate,

full of mystic significance." With this power
he could again take his place before the people as at least the equal of Philip. The multitudes would wonder at him, and acclaim him
again as "the great power of God"![1]

Objection 18:

Paul did speak about the gifts of the Spirit in 1 Corinthians 12, but he concluded by saying, *"And yet I show
you a more excellent way"* (verse 31). This means that
while tongues were temporarily in the early Church,
Paul now would have them discard the gift and choose
a more excellent way—the way of love.

Answer:

If that was Paul's intent in writing 1 Corinthians 12,
his words certainly contradict it. He began the chapter by telling the people he did not want them to be
ignorant *"concerning spiritual gifts"* (verse 1). He did not
downgrade the gifts but said that God desires that they

should be manifested through everyone (verse 7). He followed this by listing the gifts.

Paul did not conclude the chapter by implying that the gifts were temporarily useful and that now they should be discarded in favor of love (verse 31). The gifts and the fruits are not in competition; they supplement one another. It is ridiculous to say that these statements should cancel out everything else Paul said. Chapter 14 sums it up with, *"Pursue love, and desire spiritual gifts"* (verse 1). Surely, this statement cannot mean the exact opposite of what it says!

Objection 19:

Love is the only genuine evidence of the baptism in the Holy Spirit, not speaking in other tongues.

Answer:

While it is true that speaking in other tongues can be counterfeited, so can love. There is so-called physical love, which in a moment can turn to hatred and murder (2 Samuel 13:15). On the other hand, the disciples immediately knew that the people at Cornelius' house had received the Holy Spirit, *"For they heard them speak with tongues and magnify God"* (Acts 10:46). It is true that some who receive the Spirit fail to walk in the Spirit, and thus discredit their experience, as did some in the Corinthian church. But that is a different matter.

Objection 20:

The Pentecostal message primarily appeals to the ignorant and illiterate. Some critics say that Pentecostal ministers are merely appealing to human emotion and are obviously quite proficient at mass psychology, especially when directed toward the backward or uneducated types of people.

Answer:

To imply that those having the Pentecostal experience include only the ignorant and uneducated is false. Not all Pentecostal ministers have had the advantage of a college education, and many people they are serving are common people. The rulers of the Jews even held this against the apostles (Acts 4:13).

Many people without a college education became well-educated. Abraham Lincoln was such an example. Peter and John must also have done so, for the books they wrote in later years are not only well written but changed multitudes of lives. Today, many who have received the baptism in the Holy Spirit are college graduates and professionals and speak in tongues.

Objection 21:

In 1 Corinthians 14:20, Paul suggests that the gift of tongues was for the Church only during the days of its infancy. The Church received the gift of tongues in the beginning, but it was not intended to become a permanent part of the worship service.

Answer:

Although this is the position taken by those who oppose the Pentecostal experience, it certainly does not represent the position of the Scriptures. The apostle Paul said, *"I thank my God I speak with tongues more than you all"* (1 Corinthians 14:18). Is he, therefore, to be considered immature or a babe? What would be their attitude if they found that when Paul came to their church, he spoke in tongues more than all others?

Objection 22:

No responsible leaders of the historic churches believe in speaking in other tongues.

Answer:

That statement is not valid. Actually, many responsible, learned people from historic churches are now speaking and writing in favor of the experience.

Objection 23:

Speaking in other tongues is merely psychic exclamations by people who are in a state of delirium or religious frenzy.

Answer:

To this, we must sharply object. The Scriptures declare that the apostles spoke in other tongues as the Spirit gave them utterance. Therefore, to attribute such utterance to strong, psychic exclamations is dangerously close to the sin of attributing the work of the Holy Spirit to that of Beelzebub—a sin for which there is no forgiveness (Matthew 12:24-32).

The inspired writer of Acts said that speaking in other tongues came forth as the Spirit gave utterance. That is the true explanation of the glossolalia as found among those who have received the baptism in the Spirit.

Objection 24:

Speaking in other tongues is gibberish, unintelligible babbling that does not follow the rules of any known language. Others who speak in tongues appear to have nothing but stammering lips.

Answer:

The great majority who publicly speak in other tongues speak fluently, and sometimes do so in several languages. Often, each language is strikingly different from the others spoken. The actual gift mentioned by Paul is "varieties of tongues" (1 Corinthians 12:28). Some dialects, however, are very basic and may sound like gibberish, but are definite languages.

In some instances, people who have just received the baptism in the Spirit may initially speak awkwardly. They usually come forth later with a clear tongue. While no one with a stammering tongue should attempt to use it in public ministry, the Scriptures do not disown even this (Isaiah 28:11-12).

Objection 25:

Why do some people speak with stammering lips? If God has all power, should not the gift He gives be clear and perfect?

Answer:

We have to let God give the rules. The Holy Spirit does not overwhelm anyone and force them to speak in tongues. It is not unusual for people to stammer when they first begin speaking in other tongues. After fully yielding to the Spirit, they speak with a clear tongue. Stammering lips may be a stumbling block to some listeners, noted by Isaiah who says, *"Yet they would not hear"* (Isaiah 28:12).

Objection 26:

People with lives that fail to measure up to Christian standards may claim to speak in other tongues. Surely, God would not pour out His Spirit upon people who are so imperfect.

Answer:

Peter preached to people on the Day of Pentecost who had committed the greatest sin of all time—murdering the Son of God (Acts 2:22-23). Yet Peter offered these sinners the promise of the Holy Spirit upon their repentance and acceptance of the Gospel (Acts 2:38-39). Peter quoted from Joel 2:28-32, saying that God would pour out His Spirit upon *all flesh*.

Paul declared people occasionally used the gifts improperly, but he never challenged the genuineness of the gifts. Instead, he sharply reproved them for their moral negligence.

Objection 27:

Some people who speak in tongues live a lower Christian standard. Is it not presumptuous for Pentecostals to claim they have the Holy Spirit, while some of the world's leading soul winners, who have won thousands to Christ, do not have the experience?

Answer:

Those who raise this objection forget that most denominations claim that their congregants not only were saved but also received the Holy Spirit when they became members of their church. Pentecostals teach that the baptism in the Spirit is subsequent to salvation.

While it is true that every Spirit-filled person ought to live an exemplary Christian life, and it is serious not to do so, Scriptures do not indicate this will always be the case. Carnal Corinthians received the Holy Spirit because they believed it was for them, not because they were exemplary Christians.

Objection 28:

Even though speaking in other tongues is scriptural, it causes too many problems in the church. Note the difficulties Paul faced with those who spoke in tongues in the Corinthian church. Considering all these problems and complications, would it not be safer to eliminate it altogether?

Answer:

This is man's solution to the matter, not God's. The fact is that preaching and spreading the Gospel has always involved problems. When believers in the early centuries professed Christianity, it often led to martyrdom. Surely, that was a problem! A compromise was to worship both Christ and Caesar. Many chose death instead.

Naturally, some do not want to be bothered with problems; therefore, it is easier to forbid speaking in tongues. That is one way to get rid of problems, but it is not God's way (1 Thessalonians 5:19-20).

Objection 29:

If speaking in other tongues accompanies the full experience of the baptism in the Holy Spirit, why did no one speak in tongues during the centuries prior to the 20th century?

Answer:

The Bible shows that speaking in other tongues was not a phenomenon that occurred only on the Day of Pentecost and shortly after, and then ceased. Toward the end of Paul's ministry, he laid his hands on some disciples and they spoke in tongues (Acts 19:1-6).

History records the supernatural ministry of the early Church declined rapidly after the death of John. Nevertheless, the gifts of the Spirit, including speaking in other tongues, continued to manifest in some degree during the early centuries and throughout the entire church age.

Objection 30:

Speaking in other tongues, as practiced by the Pentecostals, has its source in sorcery and demon activity.

Answer:

It is true that there are false prophets, including spiritists who speak under the unction of a power other than the Spirit of God. There were false prophets in Bible days, and there are false prophets today. No Christian should turn against any of the gifts of the Holy Spirit as clearly outlined in the Bible, specifically speaking in other tongues, simply because Satan has tried to counterfeit it through the mouths of false prophets and spiritualists. On the contrary, we should not ignorant of Satan's devices (Matthew 10:16).

NOTES

1   Carl Brumback, *"What Meaneth This?"* (Springfield, MO: Gospel Publishing House, 1947), 206.

CONCLUSION

The gifts of the Holy Spirit are God's love-gifts to the Church and through the operation of these gifts, the Church becomes the functioning Body of Christ on earth. After the Holy Spirit was poured out, it became possible for Christ to manifest Himself through an unlimited number of believers. Christ ministers His love and compassion through His Body by the power of the Holy Spirit.

Jesus gave the Great Commission as a command to believers for the evangelization of the world—to be accomplished through preaching the Gospel with accompanying miraculous signs manifested through the gifts of the Spirit. These gifts confirm the Gospel.

A number of the gifts are especially designed to bring supernatural provision and deliverance to God's people in times of crisis. Certain gifts also have the definite purpose of edifying the Body of Christ so that the Church may be perfected and made ready for the second coming of Christ.

ABOUT GORDON LINDSAY

Gordon Lindsay was born in 1906, in Zion City, Illinois. At age 19, he was born again under the preaching of the evangelist, Charles Parham, in John G. Lake's church. He immediately knew that God had called him to preach the gospel and felt a strong desire to reach the multitudes but did not know how. One year after his conversion, Gordon, with two of his friends, launched into evangelistic ministry using a tent borrowed from John G. Lake. For the next ten years he confidently preached God's Word on healing and deliverance in more than 150 evangelistic crusades. After his marriage to Freda Schimpf, a convert at one of his evangelistic campaigns, they pastored several churches for the following ten years as well as continuing to preach and teach in healing revivals across the country.

Gordon took his first trip to Israel in 1947 and tirelessly worked to spread the Gospel in Israel, establishing the Jerusalem Center, a Chapel on the Mount of Olives, and publishing books and gospel tracts for distribution to both Jews and Arabs. By early 1967, it was evident that the ministry of the *Voice of Healing* had grown far beyond just the monthly magazine and the healing revivals and conventions hosted in the United States. To reflect the expansion and worldwide activity of the organization, the name was changed to Christ For The Nations.

In September 1970, Gordon launched the Christ For The Nations Institute. He had witnessed God supernaturally heal and deliver multiplied thousands, and he wanted to train and equip students to fulfill the Great Commission, reaching all ages, all classes, and all races with the supernatural power of the Gospel. On

April 1, 1973, almost three years after he birthed Christ For The Nations Institute, Gordon went home to be with the Lord, as he sat on the stage in the Institute building in a Sunday service.

Gordon Lindsay had served as an evangelist, church-planter, pastor, author, entrepreneur, apostolic leader, and teacher. He left his footprints around the world: in evangelistic crusades and conferences; through financial help to churches, Bible Schools and orphanages; and in literature through 250 books and scores of articles published in the monthly magazine. He summarized the pursuit of his life in this statement, *"The power of the gospel has not abated, nor has the Great Commission that Christ gave been changed."* In fulfilment of the dream God put in his heart when he got saved, Gordon lived to see the transforming power of the Gospel bring salvation, healing, and deliverance to multitudes in every nation of the world.

In the Right Hands, This Book Will Change Lives!

Most of the people who need this message will not be looking for this book. To change their lives, you need to **put a copy of this book in their hands.**

Our ministry is constantly seeking methods to find the people who need this anointed message to change their lives. **Will you help us reach these people?**

Extend this ministry by sowing three, five, ten, or *even more* books today and change people's lives for the better! Your generosity will be part of catalyzing the Great Awakening that many have been prophesying and praying for.

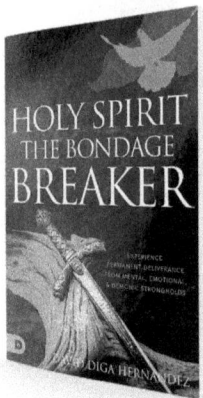

YOUR Prophetic COMMUNITY

Sign up for a **FREE** subscription to the Destiny Image digital magazine and get awesome content delivered directly to your inbox!

destinyimage.com/signup

Sign up for Cutting-Edge Messages that Supernaturally Empower You

- Gain valuable insights and guidance based on biblical principles
- Deepen your faith and understanding of God's plan for your life
- Receive regular updates and prophetic messages
- Connect with a community of believers who share your values and beliefs

Experience Fresh Video Content that Reveals Your Prophetic Inheritance

- Receive prophetic messages and insights
- Connect with a powerful tool for spiritual growth and development
- Stay connected and inspired on your faith journey

Listen to Powerful Podcasts that Propel You into God's Presence Every Day

- Deepen your understanding of God's prophetic assignment
- Experience God's revival power throughout your day
- Learn how to grow spiritually in your walk with God

From

David Diga Hernandez

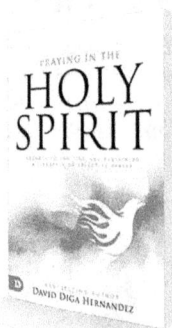

Check out
our **Destiny Image**
bestsellers page at
destinyimage.com/bestsellers

for cutting-edge,
prophetic messages
that will supernaturally
empower you and the
body of Christ.

From

Corey Russell

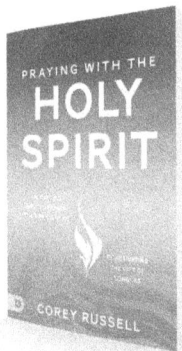

Unlock Realms of Glory through Praying in Tongues!

Is your vision of praying in tongues too small? Is it unbiblical?

Too often we, as believers, avoid praying in tongues due to confusion or misunderstanding. Yet we've unknowingly laid aside one of the most powerful tools in our spiritual arsenal. This gift brings us out of the flesh and into the Spirit—enabling us to pray from a position of victory, rout the spiritual forces of darkness, and experience a richer relationship with the Lord.

In *Praying with the Holy Spirit,* Corey Russell, a key intercessor and leader, shows you how to activate this supernatural gift, opening up new depths of intimacy with God and igniting you to pray with unshakable fervency, authority, and confidence against any enemy scheme.

Based on his bestselling book *The Glory Within*, this 40-day guided devotional journal takes you on a life-changing journey into the heart of what it means to pray in tongues—and how to do it effectively.

Don't settle for a powerless prayer life. It's time to engage the Spirit, unlock new realms of glory, and unleash the supernatural power of praying in tongues in your world.

Purchase your copy wherever books are sold

www.ingramcontent.com/pod-product-compliance
Lightning Source LLC
Chambersburg PA
CBHW061155040426
42445CB00013B/1685